Published by Creative Education
123 South Broad Street, Mankato, Minnesota 56001
Creative Education is an imprint of The Creative Company

Designed by Stephanie Blumenthal

Photographs by JLM Visuals (J. C. Cokendolpher),
KAC Productions (Kathy Adams Clark, Bill Drake),
Robert McCaw, Joe McDonald, Tom Stack & Associates
(Larry Dech, Brian Parker, Milton Rand, John Shaw)

Library of Congress Cataloging-in-Publication Data

Halfmann, Janet.
Spiders / Janet Halfmann.
p. cm. — (Let's investigate)
Includes index.
ISBN 1-58341-195-X
1. Spiders—Juvenile literature. [1. Spiders.] I. Title. II. Series.
QL458.4 .H33   2001
595.4'4—dc21   00-064497

First edition

2 4 6 8 9 7 5 3 1

Published by Creative Education
123 South Broad Street, Mankato, Minnesota 56001
Creative Education is an imprint of The Creative Company

Designed by Stephanie Blumenthal

Photographs by JLM Visuals (J. C. Cokendolpher),
KAC Productions (Kathy Adams Clark, Bill Drake),
Robert McCaw, Joe McDonald, Tom Stack & Associates
(Larry Dech, Brian Parker, Milton Rand, John Shaw)

Library of Congress Cataloging-in-Publication Data

Halfmann, Janet.
Spiders / Janet Halfmann.
p. cm. — (Let's investigate)
Includes index.
ISBN 1-58341-195-X
1. Spiders—Juvenile literature. [1. Spiders.] I. Title. II. Series.
QL458.4 .H33   2001
595.4'4—dc21   00-064497

First edition

2 4 6 8 9 7 5 3 1

SPIDERS

JANET HALFMANN

Creative Education

SPIDER
LEGEND

An ancient Greek legend tells how Arachne challenged Athena to a weaving contest. Arachne won and was turned into a spider by Athena. From Arachne comes the word *"**arachnid**."*

Long before dinosaurs roamed the earth, spiders were hunting and trapping insects. Spiders are one of the world's most successful animals. They can live just about anywhere and have two powerful tools: silk and poison. Some people are fascinated by the spider's webs and hunting skills, but others shudder at the mere thought of a spider.

SPIDER

In 1876, an elegant silk gown made from thousands of spider-webs was presented to the Queen of England. The dress was a gift from the Chinese ambassador.

5

Left, a black and yellow garden spider resting in the middle of its web Far left, the banded garden spider

SPIDER
GIANT

The largest spider is the Goliath birdeater, a tarantula from South America. Its outstretched legs would nearly cover a dinner plate.

A green lynx spider

SPIDERS AS ARACHNIDS

A spider is a small, eight-legged animal that spins silk and almost always has a poisonous bite. Spiders are not insects, but arachnids, a group that also includes scorpions, harvestmen (also called daddy longlegs), mites, and ticks. Spiders differ in several ways from insects. They have eight legs and two-part bodies, while insects have six legs and bodies that are divided into three parts. Most insects also have wings and antennae, or feelers, but spiders do not.

There are 35,000 known **species** of spiders, but thousands more are thought to exist. Spiders fit into two basic groups: hunting spiders, those that go looking for animals to eat, and web-spinning spiders, those that build silk webs to trap their food.

SPIDER
NAMES

Baboon, cat-leg, monkey, bird-eating, crab, and horse are types of tarantulas found in different parts of the world.

Above, a striped knee tarantula
Top left, a crab spider with wasp prey
Bottom left, a funnel-web spider retrieving a caught grasshopper

Fisher, or raft, spiders dart without sinking across streams and lakes around the world. They catch insects trapped in the water and also snare small fish, tadpoles, and water bugs.

8

Spiders live on every continent except Antarctica. They occupy virtually every kind of **habitat**, from rain forests and deserts to mountaintops and houses. Most species live on land, but a few make their homes in water. Spiders generally live a year or less, but female tarantulas can survive for 20 years.

A fisher spider emerging from the water

The bodies of most spiders are shorter than a paper clip. Most spiders have eight eyes, but some have six or fewer. The eyes of web-spinning spiders are small, and they can't see well. Hunting spiders may have eyes of different sizes, and some of them can be quite large. This gives hunting spiders sharp vision.

Touch is often the most important sense for spiders. Thousands of sensitive hairs cover their legs and bodies, telling them what's going on around them. Special hollow hairs even let spiders taste with their feet.

SPIDER
CHANGE

The goldenrod crab spider is normally white but changes to yellow when it sits on a yellow flower. The change takes about 24 hours.

9

Above, a brown recluse spider
Left, the goldenrod crab spider is well camouflaged as it sits on a golden bean blossom

SPIDER
HUTS

In China, farmers build little straw huts beside their rice fields for spiders to use during the winter. That way, in the spring, the spiders are ready to attack the swarms of insects that would damage the rice.

Right, a crab spider eating its prey
Below, the ornamented orb weaver

A SPIDER'S POISON

Spiders are important **predators** of insects. Every year they kill and eat 200 trillion insects, many of which harm plants or may cause diseases. Some spiders also eat baby birds, frogs, mice, or fish, and lots of spiders often eat other spiders.

A spider overpowers its **prey** with two needle-sharp **fangs**, attached to poison glands. The fangs are at the tip of the spider's strong jaws, called chelicerae (kuh-LIS-uh-ree). The spider's poisonous bite quickly kills or paralyzes its prey. Two short structures called pedipalps near the spider's mouth help it hold onto its prey.

The spider's **venom** is meant for insects, but sometimes humans get in the way. Only a few species of spiders have poison that's dangerous to people. Among the best known are widow spiders, found around the world.

SPIDER
FANGS

The fangs of most spiders swing together sideways, like pincers, to bite prey. But tarantulas can move their fangs only up and down. First they raise their heads, then they strike downward to stab their prey.

11

The glands and fangs of a tarantula

SPIDER
ZIGZAG

Many orb weavers add a silk zigzag to the center of their webs. Scientists think they do it to mimic flowers. Both the zigzag and the flowers it imitates reflect ultraviolet light, which is invisible to humans but attracts insects.

A black and yellow garden spider retrieving prey

A SPIDER'S SILK

Spiders cannot live without silk. They make it in special glands inside their bodies, and they use it every day. Not all spider silk is the same, since each silk gland makes a different kind. Most spiders make three or four kinds of silk, and those that spin intricate webs can make seven. Different glands make silk for **draglines**, wrapping eggs, spinning dry or sticky webs, and wrapping prey.

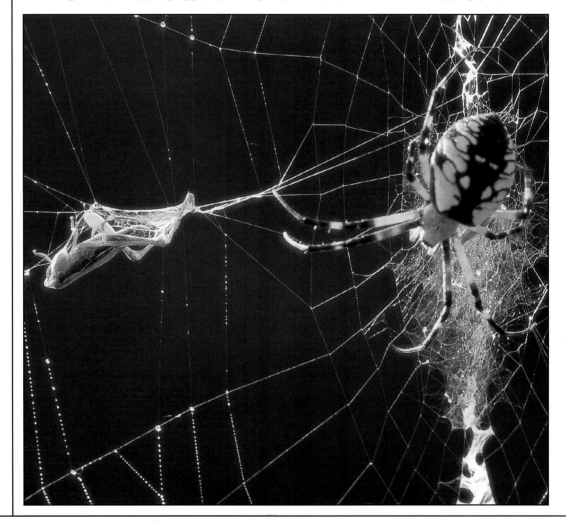

Every nine days, the world's spiders spin enough silk to reach the moon. Spider silk is so light that a silk thread long enough to circle the world would weigh less than a pound (454 g).

13

Above, a cross spider Left, an orb-weaving spider beginning to spin a web

The silk flows as a liquid from the glands to six finger-like **spinnerets** on the spider's hind end. Each spinneret has hundreds of tiny openings. The spinnerets pull and stretch the silk to turn it into solid thread. Spider silk is stronger than a steel wire of the same thickness and as flexible as a bungee cord.

SPIDER

D O O R S

Trapdoor spiders cap their silk-lined burrows with a hinged trapdoor made of silk. They wait behind the door to grab passing insects. Trapdoor spiders are related to tarantulas and live in deserts and other regions with a warm climate.

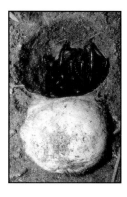

Above, an open door of a trapdoor spider
Right, a shamrock spider on a silk dragline

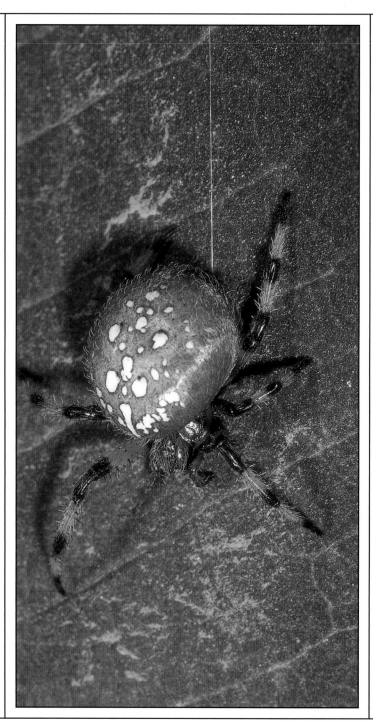

The best-known use of spider silk is to spin web traps, but only about half of all spiders make webs. All spiders, though, depend on silk to survive. One everyday use is the dragline, the silk safety line that spiders trail behind them wherever they go. They use it when dropping away from danger, leaping for insects, or finding the way home.

Every species of spider builds a nest of silk for hiding, resting, or raising its young. Some spiders spin silk linings in leaves or burrows, and others spin silk tubes or weave twigs together.

Many spiders, especially web spinners, wrap their victims in silk sheets, like mummies. Some wrap before they bite, and others wrap after. An insect mummy isn't about to escape or fight back against the spider.

Females use a lot of silk to make their **egg sacs**. They often use several kinds, putting fluffy silk near the eggs and strong, tangled silk on the outside.

The purse-web spider extends the silk lining of its burrow up the side of a tree to make a kind of purse. It bites flies and other insects right through the purse, pulls them inside, and then fixes the hole. These spiders live in North America, Europe, Asia, and Africa.

15

A star-bellied spider guarding its egg sac

SPIDER
S P I T

The spitting spider spits gummy glue from its fangs into a zigzag pattern. This sticky silk pins its victim to the ground so the spider can bite it. The night-hunting spitting spider is found around the world.

Above, spitting spider
Right, some wolf spiders reach four inches (10.2 cm) in length

HUNTING SPIDERS

The hunting spiders are wanderers who search for prey instead of building traps. Some creep up on their victims, and others lie in wait and then pounce.

Wolf spiders are hairy and swift, like wolves, but they don't hunt in packs. Two of their eyes are large, making them excellent hunters. Wolf spiders can be found around the world, running on the ground, over stones, and up plants. Some kinds dig burrows with their strong jaws.

SPIDER

BORROWERS

Jumping spiders can leap 40 times the length of their bodies. All around the world, they stalk insects the way cats do, then glue down their draglines and leap. Jumping spiders are small and chunky, with short legs. The males in hot regions are often brightly colored.

Crab spiders are ambushers. They live all around the world and perch on flowers, plants, and tree bark, waiting for insects. Bees are a favorite food, so the crab spider's poison has to work fast to keep the spider from getting stung. These dime-sized spiders look and walk like crabs.

A giant crab spider perched on a leaf

18

SPIDER

TRAVELERS

Jumping spiders have been found at 22,000 feet (6,700 m) on Mount Everest, higher than any other animal. The spiders feed on tiny creatures that live on plants carried up the mountain by the wind.

The huge, hairy tarantulas are the world's largest spiders. The biggest ones live in the rain forests of South America. Some, such as the pink-toed tarantula, live in trees and are big enough to capture baby birds. Most tarantulas live in silk-lined burrows in the ground. In warm areas around the world, they creep out at night to hunt insects. Most tarantulas shy away from people and have a bite no worse than a wasp sting.

Above, a male bowl and doily spider
Left, the white-footed tarantula of Central America

SPIDER
TRIANGLE

The tiny triangle spider builds a web shaped like a triangle. When an insect hits the web, the spider springs it like a trap, entangling the victim. This is one of the few spiders without a poisonous bite.

WEB-SPINNING SPIDERS

Spiders that spin webs use traps to catch their food because they can't see well. Some webs are tinier than a postage stamp, and others span streams and small rivers.

The tangled-web weavers spin simple, untidy webs, commonly called cobwebs. These jumbles of silk are often found attached to the walls and ceilings of houses. Cellar spiders spin their tangled webs in basements and other dark places around the world. Also common are cobweb or comb-footed spiders, whose family includes the widow spiders, which are dangerous to humans. Comb-footed spiders throw sticky silk over their victims using a hair comb on their legs.

A female dictynid spider crawling in her web

The Piaroa Indians of Venezuela feast on roasted tarantulas. They use the fangs as toothpicks to pick the spiders' hard outer shells from their teeth. In Southeast Asia, people eat large, hairy barbecued spiders on a stick.

The sheet-web weavers spin flat sheets of silk stretched between blades of grass or between the branches of shrubs or trees. The sheets often look like little hammocks or bowls, and they can carpet a large area. Threads above the sheet snag insects, which bounce onto the sheet. The spider waits beneath the sheet and pulls the insects through it. An example is the bowl and doily spider, found throughout Canada and the United States. Many of the tinier sheet-web weavers are known as dwarf spiders. In Great Britain these are called money spiders, because some people believe they bring money or other good fortune.

Above, a red-legged tarantula
Left, a bowl and doily spider web

SPIDER

In France and Spain, cobweb spiders are sometimes put into wine cellars to eat the insects that bore into wine corks.

The web of a funnel-weaving spider

The funnel-web spiders weave horizontal webs that include a funnel, or tube, for a hiding place. The spider hides in the funnel with its legs outstretched. When its legs feel an insect walking on the web, the spider rushes out and bites it. European house spiders, found around the world, are some of the best-known funnel weavers. They build their webs in bathrooms and other dark, moist places. When the males go looking for mates, they often fall into bathtubs. Then they can't get out because the sides of the tub are too slippery.

The orb weavers are found around the world. They spin orbs, or **spirals**, which are the best-known and most beautiful of all spiderwebs. Some orb weavers lie in wait for their prey in the center of the web. Others attach a signal line that leads to a nest near the web. The beautiful orange-brown European garden spider is probably the most familiar orb weaver.

SPIDER
NETS

Golden silk spiders live in hot climates. They spin golden webs so large and strong that they can trap birds. Local people sometimes use the webs for fishing nets.

23

Left, a shamrock spider and its orb web full of morning dew
Below, red-spotted crab spider and prey

SPIDER
ENGINEER

Right, a very large and beautiful orb web
Far right, a nursery web spider

SPINNING AN ORB WEB

Most orb weavers build a new web every 24 hours, usually at night. The largest webs are made by the females. The European garden spider begins its web by letting a thread of silk flutter in the wind until it sticks to a twig. This thread, stretched between two twigs, forms the top of the web's frame. The spider then adds more frame lines and about 30 spokes, which are positioned like the spokes in a bicycle wheel.

Next, starting from the center, the spider spins a temporary spiral of dry silk. That done, it retraces its steps, eating the dry silk and replacing it with a tight spiral of sticky silk. The spider jerks each thread to break its sticky coating into beads, like a little necklace. In less than an hour, the trap is ready to catch prey.

SPIDER WOMAN

According to Navajo legend, a young girl was taught the secrets of weaving by Spider Woman, who said that a hole representing her burrow must be left in each woven item. Such a hole can still be found in many Navajo blankets today.

25

SPIDER BABIES

Most spiders live alone, except when they mate. After mating, the males soon die, and the females get ready to lay their eggs. First the female spins a disk of silk. On this, she lays her eggs, covers them with silk, and bundles them into a protective silk sac.

The average-sized female spider lays about 100 eggs. Large spiders can lay 2,000 or more. Some spider species take care of their eggs and babies, but most hide their egg sacs in a protected place and die soon afterward.

SPIDER KISS

Contrary to popular belief, female spiders, including the black widow, don't usually eat their mates. But a few types do. The female pallid garden spider, holding the tiny male in her jaws in order to mate, ends up eating him.

A black and yellow garden spider guarding its egg sac

SPIDER

COURTSHIP

Male spiders tend to be much smaller than females. To make sure the female doesn't mistake him for a meal, the male puts on a show. Male jumping spiders dance, the nursery web spider brings a silk-wrapped fly, and orb weavers pluck their mates' webs like a harp.

Right, spiderlings in nest
Below, a spider ready to lay eggs

Inside the sac, the eggs hatch into babies called spiderlings. The spiderlings **molt** once, then wait for warm weather before breaking out of their sac. The babies may stay together for a while, then soon spread out. Some walk to new places, but many spiderlings that are born outdoors travel by **ballooning**. They climb to high spots and let out strands of silk. The wind catches the silk and carries the spiderlings near and far.

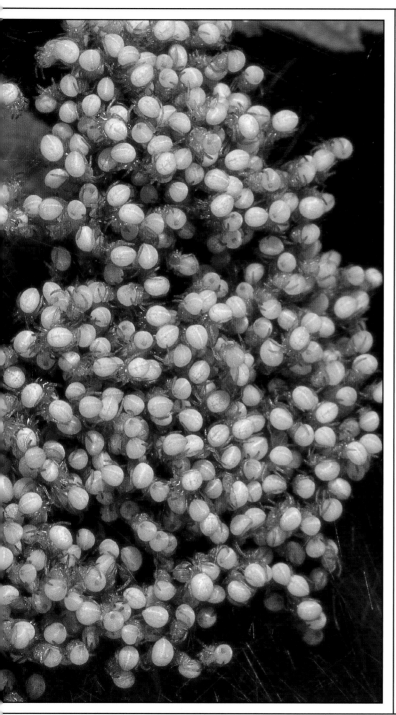

From the day they emerge from the sac, most spiderlings take care of themselves. They know how to use their silk and poison to capture food and to escape frogs, birds, and other enemies. The spiderlings molt several more times on their way to becoming adults. Eventually they mate, and soon clouds of new spiderlings balloon across the sky.

SPIDER
MOTHERS

The female wolf spider attaches her egg sac to her spinnerets, and later a hundred or more babies ride on her back. Nursery web spiders carry their egg sacs in their jaws and build a silken tent for the newly hatched babies.

Above, a wolf spider with its egg sac

SPIDER
MEDICINE

Long ago, doctors prescribed a spider hung in a bag around the neck or swallowed with bread to relieve fever. Spiderwebs were used on wounds to stop bleeding.

SPIDER
SCIENCE

Today, scientists are studying spider venoms to see if they can be used to treat heart attacks and relieve pain. Someday, doctors may even use spider silk to stitch wounds.

The stretch spider does not spin a web

SPIDERS AND PEOPLE

Spiders are both loved and hated. People admire them for eating insects and for spinning artistic webs, but many people are frightened by their long, hairy legs and secretive lives. In many cultures, people consider it unlucky to kill a spider. Even people who don't like spiders often can't bring themselves to kill one. Many cultures tell tales of heroes helped by spiders. On the other hand, the Old English word for spider means "poison-head."

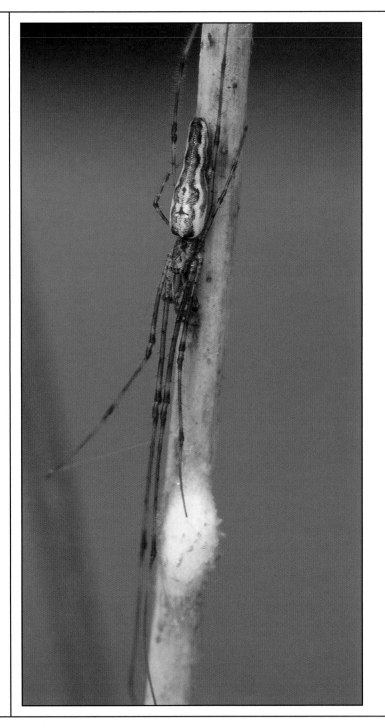

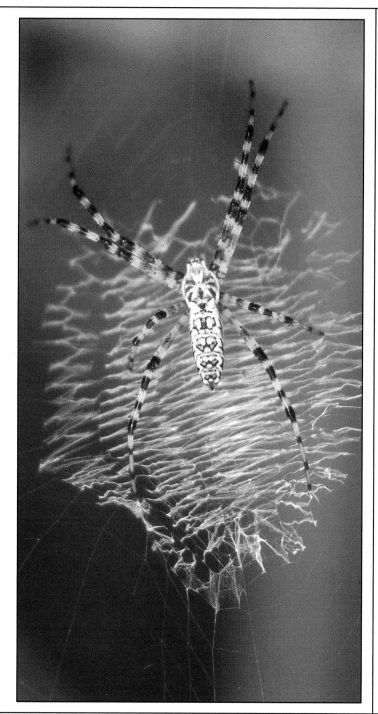

O ften, the more people learn about spiders, the less likely they are to fear them. When they find a spiderweb, taking a minute to watch its little weaver from a safe distance offers a glimpse at a fascinating creature and one of nature's great artists.

SPIDER
S P A C E

Two European garden spiders were aboard Skylab II to test web building in space. Although it took a while for the spiders to adjust to weight-lessness, their webs differed little from what they would have spun on Earth.

Above, a small variety of garden spider
Left, a scaled spider

Glossary

An **arachnid** (uh-RACK-nid) is any of a group of animals having four pairs of legs, two-part bodies, and no wings or antennae.

When they float through the air using silk threads, baby spiders are **ballooning**.

Draglines are the silk threads that a spider attaches to surfaces to support it when it leaps or falls.

Egg sacs are the protective silk cases female spiders build around their eggs.

Fangs are the needle-sharp parts of the spider's jaw through which the spider injects poison into its prey.

A **habitat** is the place where an animal or plant naturally lives and grows.

For a spider to grow, it needs to **molt**, or shed its hard outer shell. A new, larger skin is underneath.

Predators are animals that capture other animals for food. Animals captured for food are **prey**.

A **species** is a group of closely related animals that can mate with one another.

The **spinnerets** are nozzles attached to the spider's silk glands. Hundreds of spigots on the spinnerets control the thickness of the spider's silk threads and combine the threads.

Spirals are curves that keep winding outward around their center.

The liquid poison produced by spiders is called **venom**.

Index